Celebrity Bios

SELENA GOMEZ

Susan Johnston Taylor

WWW.APEXEDITIONS.COM

Copyright © 2025 by Apex Editions, Mendota Heights, MN 55120. All rights reserved. No part of this book may be reproduced or utilized in any form or by any means without written permission from the publisher.

Apex is distributed by North Star Editions:
sales@northstareditions.com | 888-417-0195

Produced for Apex by Red Line Editorial.

Photographs ©: Sthanlee B. Mirador/Sipa USA/AP Images, cover, 1; Rich Fury/Invision/AP Images, 4–5, 6–7; Shutterstock Images, 8–9, 14–15, 16–17, 24–25, 28–29, 37, 38–39, 46–47, 58; Arlene Richie/The Chronicle Collection/Getty Images, 10–11; Donna McWilliam/AP Images, 12–13; Jordan Strauss/Invision/AP Images, 18–19; Paul Hiffmeyer/Disney/Getty Images Entertainment/Getty Images, 20–21; Chris Pizzello/AP Images, 22–23; Chris Pizzello/Invision/AP Images, 26–27, 56–57; Christopher Polk/TAS/Getty Images Entertainment/Getty Images, 30–31; Lester Cohen/Getty Images Entertainment/Getty Images, 32–33; Evan Agostini/Invision/AP Images, 34–35; Parisa Afsahi/Sipa USA/AP Images, 40–41; Cindy Ord/Getty Images Entertainment/Getty Images, 42–43; BauerGriffin/MediaPunch/IPx/AP Images, 44–45; Xavier Collin/Image Press Agency/Sipa USA/AP Images, 49, 52–53; Matt Sayles/Invision/AP Images, 50–51; Richard Shotwell/Invision/AP Images, 54–55

Library of Congress Control Number: 2023924697

ISBN
979-8-89250-220-7 (hardcover)
979-8-89250-241-2 (paperback)
979-8-89250-281-8 (ebook pdf)
979-8-89250-262-7 (hosted ebook)

Printed in the United States of America
Mankato, MN
082024

NOTE TO PARENTS AND EDUCATORS

Apex books are designed to build literacy skills in striving readers. Exciting, high-interest content attracts and holds readers' attention. The text is carefully leveled to allow students to achieve success quickly.

TABLE OF CONTENTS

Chapter 1
STAGE SENSATION 4

Chapter 2
A STAR IS BORN 8

Chapter 3
A CHILD STAR GROWS UP 16

Chapter 4
COMEBACK QUEEN 26

In the Spotlight
JULY MOON 36

Chapter 5
NEW PROJECTS 38

In the Spotlight
SHOWING STRUGGLES 48

Chapter 6
LASTING SUCCESS 51

FAST FACTS • 59
COMPREHENSION QUESTIONS • 60
GLOSSARY • 62
TO LEARN MORE • 63
ABOUT THE AUTHOR • 63
INDEX • 64

Chapter 1

STAGE SENSATION

Thousands of fans pack an arena. Selena Gomez steps onto the stage. A wind machine blows her hair. Her outfit sparkles. She sings her hit song "Who Says." It's about being beautiful just as you are.

Selena Gomez performed 54 shows across 10 countries on her 2016 Revival Tour.

During the Revival Tour, Gomez performed 20 songs at each show.

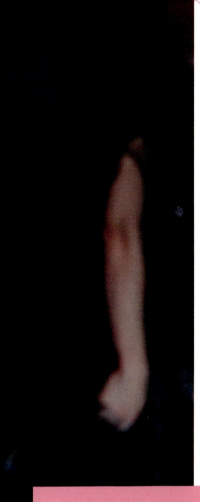

Gomez speaks to the audience. She tells them to love themselves and have confidence. Her fans cheer. They call themselves Selenators. Gomez's kindness inspires them. So does her honesty. They hope to be like her one day.

SPEAKING UP AND SINGING OUT

"Who Says" sold millions of copies. But Gomez almost didn't get to sing it. Her record label planned to give the song to another artist. However, Gomez loved the song's message. She fought to sing it herself.

Chapter 2

A STAR IS BORN

Selena Gomez was born on July 22, 1992. She grew up in Grand Prairie, Texas. Selena's parents split up when she was five. Selena mostly lived with her mom. She spent some weekends and holidays with her dad.

Grand Prairie is a city near Dallas, Texas.

Selena Quintanilla was the first Latina artist with a No. 1 album on the Billboard 200 chart.

When Selena was young, her mom worked several jobs. One was as a makeup artist. Selena played with the extra makeup. Selena's mom also did some acting. Selena wanted to try acting, too. So, she auditioned for a TV show. It was called *Barney & Friends*.

ANOTHER SELENA

Selena Gomez's grandparents were immigrants. They moved to the United States from Mexico. Selena's dad named her after a famous Tejano singer. The singer's name was Selena Quintanilla. When Selena Gomez grew up, she became a fan of the singer, too.

Barney & Friends was a popular show on PBS Kids. New episodes aired from 1992 to 2010.

Selena got the part on *Barney & Friends*. In 2002, she started filming. She played a girl named Gianna. Next, Selena got a small movie part. *Spy Kids 3-D: Game Over* came out in 2003. The movie was about a kid saving his sister who is trapped in a game. Selena played a side character.

MEETING A FRIEND

Demi Lovato was on *Barney & Friends*. Demi and Selena met at the auditions. They were the same age and became friends. Later, both became Disney stars. They co-starred in the TV movie *Princess Protection Program*.

Selena was one of the highest-paid child actors. She reportedly earned $30,000 per episode of *Wizards of Waverly Place*.

After *Spy Kids*, Selena had a few small TV appearances. Then, when she was 15, Selena got her big break. She landed the lead role on *Wizards of Waverly Place*. It was a major Disney TV show. The show was about a wizard family. Selena played the middle child, Alex.

MEXICAN PRIDE

Alex on *Wizards of Waverly Place* was Mexican American. Selena is, too. The show featured Mexican traditions such as the *quinceañera*. That event celebrates a young woman's 15th birthday. Mexican American fans liked seeing their culture on TV.

15

Chapter 3

A CHILD STAR GROWS UP

Wizards of Waverly Place shot Selena Gomez to fame. The show was a huge success. Selena played Alex for four years. She filmed more than 100 episodes. She even sang the theme song.

Wizards of Waverly Place: The Movie came out in 2009.

Wizards led to many new projects. Selena appeared on the Disney show *Hannah Montana*. She filmed several movies, too. *Another Cinderella Story* came out in 2008. It was a modern version of Cinderella. *Ramona and Beezus* came out in 2010. It was about two sisters. Selena played the big sister, Beezus.

A SWIFT FRIENDSHIP

Selena and Taylor Swift met in 2008. They were first seen together at the release of *Another Cinderella Story*. The two became good friends. As of 2024, they were still close.

Selena Gomez and Taylor Swift have attended many award shows together.

Many Disney stars begin with acting. Then they start music careers.

Selena was a successful actress. But she was interested in music, too. She had already sung songs for TV and movies. In 2008, she signed a record deal. She formed a pop-rock band. The band was called Selena Gomez & The Scene. They released their first album, *Kiss & Tell,* in 2009. The song "Naturally" became a hit.

In 2010, the band released *A Year Without Rain*. The songs are about being true to oneself. In 2011, their third album, *When the Sun Goes Down*, came out. It had dance-pop beats. Then, in 2013, Selena Gomez tried something new. She released a solo album. It made her an even bigger star.

STARS DANCE

Gomez's first solo album was her most successful yet. *Stars Dance* sold nearly 100,000 copies in its first week. It reached No. 1 on the Billboard album chart. It was her first project to reach that spot.

Gomez sang at the People's Choice Awards in 2011. Her band won an award there.

The *Hotel Transylvania* series is about a family of monsters.

Gomez's music career was doing well. But she kept acting, too. Her early projects were for young audiences. Now, she was getting older. She wanted to show new sides of herself. In 2012, she started taking on new roles. The stories were darker and more serious. Gomez did a thriller. Later, she even did a zombie movie.

VOICE ACTING

Gomez did voice acting for several animated films. She played Helga in *Horton Hears a Who*. In *Arthur 3*, she played Selenia. And she played Mavis in *Hotel Transylvania*. That movie had three sequels. Gomez was in all of them.

Chapter 4

COMEBACK QUEEN

In 2013, Gomez started a world tour. Fans loved her big smile. They danced to her upbeat music. But behind the scenes, something was wrong. Gomez felt tired and achy. She had to cancel some concerts.

Gomez's concerts often sold out. On some nights, more than 70,000 people attended.

Gomez talked with doctors. They told her she had lupus. So, she took a break from performing. She needed to focus on her health. Gomez had chemotherapy. She took other medicines. And she made some changes to her daily habits.

LUPUS

Lupus is a disease in which the body attacks itself. It affects about 1.5 million people in the United States. Each case is different. Gomez has had bad body pain. She has also had kidney problems. Often, people with lupus get rashes. Some feel very tired.

Gomez did not stop all her activities. In 2014, she attended the premiere of her movie *Rudderless*.

In 2015, Gomez was a surprise guest at one of Taylor Swift's shows.

Lupus does not have a cure. But Gomez's treatments helped. In 2015, she felt well enough to perform. She released a second solo album. It was called *Revival*. The album was very personal. "Good for You" became a popular single. So did "Same Old Love." Critics praised the album.

MENTAL HEALTH

Being in the spotlight isn't easy. Gossip blogs wrote about Gomez's life. She had mental health issues. Those can be side effects of lupus. Gomez got help for her mental health. She urged fans to get help if they need it, too.

By 2017, lupus made Gomez sicker again. She needed a new kidney. Gomez's family members got tested. They couldn't donate a kidney. But her friend Francia Raisa was a match. She gave Gomez one of her kidneys.

GIVING BACK

Charity work has always been important to Gomez. Her time in hospitals made her want to do even more. She helped raise money for lupus research. She visited sick kids, too.

Gomez and Francia Raisa (right) met in 2007.

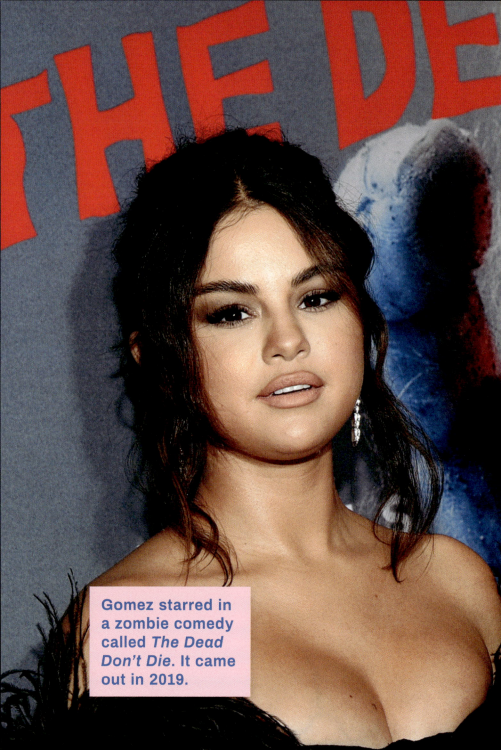

Gomez starred in a zombie comedy called *The Dead Don't Die*. It came out in 2019.

Gomez felt better a few months later. She started working again. She filmed a movie. And she released the song "Wolves" with DJ Marshmello. In 2020, she released *Rare*. It was her most personal album yet. Gomez helped write several songs. They explored love and loss.

A GOOD REMINDER

Gomez has many tattoos. One of them is the word "rare." It reminds Gomez of her value. It reminds her that she doesn't have to be perfect.

In the Spotlight

JULY MOON

Gomez doesn't just act in movies and TV shows. She also helps produce them. In 2008, Gomez and her mom created July Moon Productions. With that company, Gomez could help make projects that matter to her.

From 2017 to 2020, Gomez worked on *13 Reasons Why*. The Netflix show explored trauma and mental health. Gomez also worked on *Living Undocumented*. It was a documentary series. It told the stories of eight families. It showed what their lives were like after coming to the United States.

In the early 2020s, more than 10 million undocumented people lived in the United States.

Chapter 5
NEW PROJECTS

In 2020, Gomez shared more news with fans. She told them she has bipolar disorder. Bipolar disorder is a mental health condition. Gomez wanted to be honest. And as before, she wanted to help her fans. She showed it was okay to ask for help.

Gomez has a wide reach. By 2024, she had more than 400 million followers on Instagram.

Gomez also kept working. She made more music videos. She did more voice acting. Gomez produced more projects, too. The teen movie *This Is the Year* came out in 2020.

In 2021, Gomez recorded a new album. It was her first one all in Spanish. The album was called *Revelación*.

COOKING UP A NEW SHOW

During the COVID-19 pandemic, Gomez started a reality TV show. It was called *Selena + Chef*. On the show, famous chefs taught Gomez home cooking. In the first season, she donated $10,000 per episode. Chefs got to pick the charities.

40

Dolittle came out in 2020. It was about a doctor who can talk to animals. Gomez voiced a giraffe named Betsy.

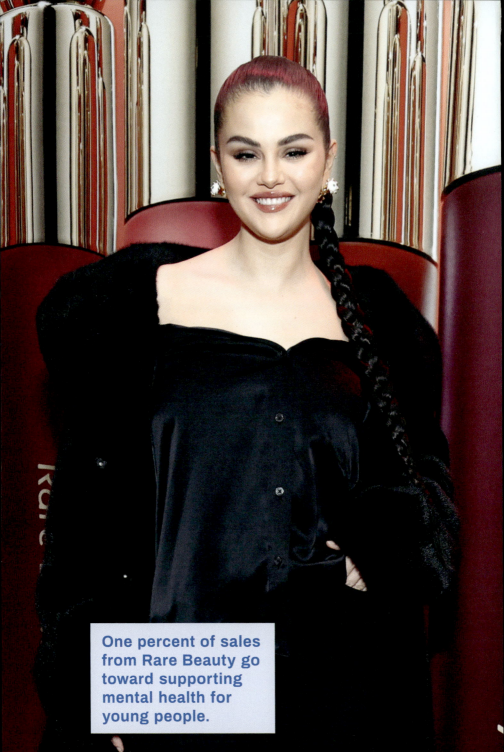

One percent of sales from Rare Beauty go toward supporting mental health for young people.

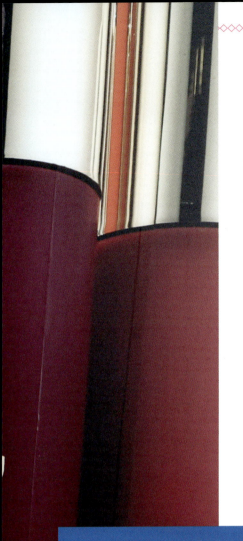

Gomez was always interested in makeup. She wanted to make a beauty brand that welcomed everyone. So, in 2020, Gomez launched one of her biggest projects ever. It was called Rare Beauty. In 2023, the beauty brand made more than $300 million.

OTHER COMPANIES

Over the years, Gomez has had many businesses. One is Wondermind. Gomez and her mom helped found it. It helps people stay mentally healthy. Gomez has released cooking products, perfumes, and clothes, too.

Martin Short (left) and Steve Martin (right) are well-known comedians.

In 2021, Gomez began a new TV show. It was called *Only Murders in the Building*. Gomez produced it. She acted in it, too. Gomez plays Mabel Mora. Someone in Mora's building gets murdered. Mora and two neighbors try to solve the crime.

ONLY MURDERS IN THE BUILDING

Gomez has two co-stars on the show. One is Martin Short. The other is Steve Martin. Both actors are famous for being funny. They have been acting together for many years.

45

Gomez was nominated for a Golden Globe in 2023 for her performance in *Only Murders in the Building*.

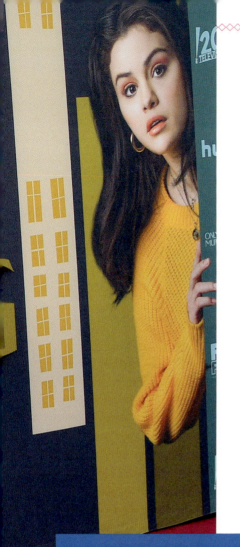

Critics loved *Only Murders*. They liked how Gomez's character changed over the seasons. Audiences loved the show, too. It became a big hit. By 2023, Gomez had filmed two more seasons.

MUSIC COLLABS

Gomez tried many projects after the pandemic. But she still made music. She released "Let Somebody Go" with Coldplay. She did "Selfish Love" with DJ Snake. In 2023, she released "Single Soon."

In the Spotlight

SHOWING STRUGGLES

For six years, a camera crew filmed Gomez's life. They captured good and bad moments. In 2022, Gomez put the footage together. She released a documentary. It was called *Selena Gomez: My Mind & Me*.

The documentary focused on her fame and mental health. It showed her hard times. For example, one scene showed Gomez crying after a performance. Gomez was very honest. Many viewers enjoyed seeing her true feelings. They felt connected to her.

> Gomez even shared journal entries in *Selena Gomez: My Mind & Me*.

By 2024, Gomez had won 12 Nickelodeon Kids' Choice Awards.

Chapter 6
LASTING SUCCESS

Some child actors stop being famous as adults. But Gomez remained a household name. She won a total of 18 Teen Choice Awards. And in 2020, *People* magazine named her a Person of the Year. Since then, she has earned several Emmy nominations.

Gomez's music earned awards, too. For example, she won two Young Hollywood Awards in 2013. Teenagers voted to choose the winners. In 2016, she won an American Music Award. Her success continued through her music career. In 2023, she won a Billboard Music Award.

GREAT VIDEOS

The MTV Video Music Awards (VMAs) honor the year's best music videos. Gomez won her first VMA in 2013. It was for "Come and Get It." Ten years later, she won another VMA. This time, it was for "Calm Down" with Rema.

Gomez attended the Video Music Awards in 2023.

Gomez became a UNICEF Ambassador in 2009. She helps children around the world.

Gomez cares deeply about her charity work. From a young age, she has used her fame to help people in need. In 2009, she recorded the song "Send It On" for Disney. The song encouraged people to take care of the planet. Gomez also promotes mental health.

DOG LOVER

In 2009, Gomez filmed a movie in Puerto Rico. She saw lots of stray dogs. So, Gomez helped raise money to help them. She even has two rescue dogs herself. One is named Daisy. The other is named Winnie.

Gomez's life has been full of ups and downs. She has had hard times. She has had great successes, too. Through it all, Gomez learned that self-love is important. She hoped her fans could always feel that, too.

WOMAN OF THE YEAR

In 2017, Billboard named Gomez its Woman of the Year. The award recognized her music. It recognized her impact, too. Billboard said Gomez inspired young women. She showed them how to use their voices and give back.

Gomez spoke emotionally when she received Billboard's Woman of the Year award.

FAST FACTS

Full name: Selena Marie Gomez
Birth date: July 22, 1992
Birthplace: Grand Prairie, Texas,
   United States of America

TIMELINE

1992	Selena Gomez is born on July 22.
2002–04	Selena films the TV show *Barney & Friends*.
2007–12	Selena Gomez stars in her breakout role, the Disney TV show *Wizards of Waverly Place*.
2009	Selena Gomez & The Scene release their first album.
2013	Gomez releases her first solo album, *Stars Dance*.
2017	Gomez gets a kidney transplant.
2017	Gomez is named Billboard's Woman of the Year.
2020	Gomez launches Rare Beauty.
2021–23	Gomez begins starring in *Only Murders in the Building*.

COMPREHENSION QUESTIONS

Write your answers on a separate piece of paper.

1. Write a few sentences explaining how Selena Gomez became famous.

2. Would you rather sing in a band, act in a movie, or be part of a TV show? Why?

3. What was Gomez's first TV acting job?
    - A. *Barney & Friends*
    - B. *Princess Protection Program*
    - C. *Wizards of Waverly Place*

4. How might Gomez's openness about her problems be helpful to fans?
    - A. Fans might be angry about her problems.
    - B. Fans might learn ways to face their own problems.
    - C. Fans might want to have the same problems.

5. What does **inspires** mean in this book?

*Gomez's kindness **inspires** them. So does her honesty. They hope to be like her one day.*

    A. makes people dislike someone
    B. makes people want to do something
    C. makes people stop listening

6. What does **immigrants** mean in this book?

*Selena Gomez's grandparents were **immigrants**. They moved to the United States from Mexico.*

    A. people who stay in one place
    B. people who move to a new country
    C. people who don't have children

Answer key on page 64.

GLOSSARY

auditioned
Tried to get an acting job.

bipolar disorder
A mental illness that can include big shifts in mood.

chemotherapy
The use of strong chemicals to treat disease.

critics
People who judge works of art such as movies and music.

documentary
A film or TV show that tells facts about real events.

nominations
Being chosen as a finalist for an award or honor.

pandemic
A time when a disease spreads quickly around the world.

produce
To help plan the making of a movie or TV show.

record label
A company that helps artists put out music.

Tejano
A music style mixing Mexican, European, and American sounds.

trauma
Painful events that cause lasting fear and shock.

undocumented
Not having the legal papers to be in a country.

TO LEARN MORE

BOOKS

Andral, Dolores. *What You Never Knew About Selena Gomez*. North Mankato, MN: Capstone Press, 2023.

Andrews, Elizabeth. *Olivia Rodrigo: Best-Selling Songwriter*. Minneapolis: Abdo Publishing, 2024.

Huddleston, Emma. *Taylor Swift*. Mendota Heights, MN: Focus Readers, 2021.

ONLINE RESOURCES

Visit **www.apexeditions.com** to find links and resources related to this title.

ABOUT THE AUTHOR

Susan Johnston Taylor lives in Austin, Texas, with her husband and two rescue dogs. Her debut picture book, *Animals in Surprising Shades: Poems About Earth's Colorful Creatures*, released in 2023. She's also part of the Paramount Story Wranglers, a professional troupe that performs songs and sketches based on students' writing.

INDEX

albums, 21–22, 30, 35, 40
Another Cinderella Story, 18
awards, 51–52, 56

Barney & Friends, 11, 13
Billboard, 22, 52, 56
bipolar disorder, 38

charity, 32, 40, 55

Disney, 13, 15, 18, 55

Hotel Transylvania, 25

July Moon Productions, 36

Living Undocumented, 36
Lovato, Demi, 13
lupus, 28, 31–32

makeup, 11, 43
Martin, Steve, 45
mental health, 31, 36, 38, 43, 48, 55

Only Murders in the Building, 45, 47

Princess Protection Program, 13

Raisa, Francia, 32
Ramona and Beezus, 18
Rare, 35
Rare Beauty, 43
Revival, 30

Selena + Chef, 40
Selena Gomez & The Scene, 21
Selena Gomez: My Mind & Me, 48
Short, Martin, 45
Spy Kids 3-D: Game Over, 13, 15
Stars Dance, 22
Swift, Taylor, 18

Texas, 8
This Is the Year, 40

ANSWER KEY:
1. Answers will vary; 2. Answers will vary; 3. A; 4. B; 5. B; 6. B